LET'S INVESTIGATE

Maps
and
Scale Drawings

LET'S INVESTIGATE

Maps
and
Scale Drawings

By Marion Smoothey
Illustrated by Ann Baum

MARSHALL CAVENDISH
NEW YORK • LONDON • TORONTO • SYDNEY

© Marshall Cavendish Corporation 1995

Published by Marshall Cavendish Corporation
2415 Jerusalem Avenue
PO Box 587
North Bellmore
New York 11710

Series created by Graham Beehag Books

Editorial consultant: Prof. Sonia Helton
University of South Florida, St. Petersburg

Library of Congress Cataloging-in-Publication Data

Smoothey, Marion,
    Maps and scale drawings / by Marion Smoothey :
    illustrated by Ann Baum. – Library ed.
       p. cm. – (Lets Investigate)
    Includes index.
    ISBN 1-85435-778-6 ISBN 1-854535-773-5 (set)
    1. Maps – Juvenile literature. [1. Maps.]
    I. Baum, Ann. ill. II. Title. III. Series: Smoothey, Marion, 1943-
    Lets Investigate.
    GA105.6.S66 1995   94-22463
    912'.014 – dc20   CIP
                            AC

Printed in Malaysia by Times Offset (M) SDN BHD

Contents

Introduction

This book will help you to understand maps, plans, and scale drawings so that you can use them yourself. You will find things to make, games to play, and puzzles to solve. In order to do all the activities, you will need paper for drawing – graph paper will be easiest to work with – a sharp pencil, a ruler, an eraser, scissors, a protractor or 45° triangle, a piece of string about two feet long, two dice, a saucer, a bar magnet, a needle and pin, a drinking straw, paper glue, some oranges, a ball, and sheets of newspaper. You might like to use a calculator but it is not essential.

Giving Directions

When someone asks you the way to a particular place, they usually expect you to explain how to get there in terms of right and left turns. If you have problems remembering which is right and which is left, it helps if you think about which hand you use to write.

Tammy lives in the town shown in the drawing on the opposite page. To get to school, she comes out of her front door, turns right, and walks along the street until she comes to a T intersection. At the intersection she turns right, walks past a shop and a house on her right, and turns right into the school drive.

● **1.** On which street does Tammy live?

Maria lives at the house with the red door. She turns right out of her house and walks as far as the hospital. She crosses the road there and takes the road that is straight ahead of her. She enters the third building on her right.

● **1.** Where has Maria gone?

Alvin and Jean have just gotten off the bus at the stop and want to know the way to the Recreation Center.

● **2.** Should they turn left or right at the end of Elm Drive?

● **3.** What directions would help someone find their way from the apartments to the nearest bus stop?

A Bird's Eye View

Ethan is lost in a maze. All he can see is tall yew hedges and a short distance along the path. He cannot see over the hedges or around the corners.

Ethan has very little idea where he is in relation to the entrance, middle, and exit of the maze. This is a map of the maze with Ethan's position marked on it.

The map is a drawing of the view of the maze that a bird or a passenger in a helicopter would see. Because you can now see where the dead ends are, it is easy to give Ethan instructions to help him find his way to the exit.

● **4.** Write down the directions, in terms of left and right, that Ethan needs to help him to escape.

● **5.** If you begin at the start, what is the most direct route to the finish? Either make a copy of the maze to draw on or write down directions in terms of left and right. You can use L and R. Do not write in the book.

Try drawing some mazes of your own and see how long it takes your friends to find the best route to the exit.

A simple map, or bird's eye view, of the roads and buildings shown on page 6 would look something like this.

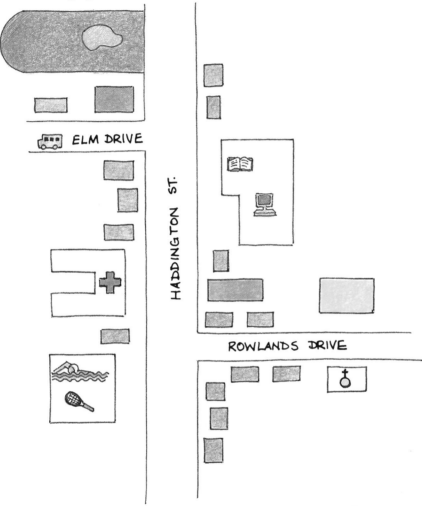

Because you see only the outline shape of the buildings and cannot see any details, a hospital looks similar to a house. If the map has to show a lot of detail in a small space, there is not enough room to label every building with its name. The problem can be overcome by using different colors for different types of buildings.

Also, features such as parks and rivers can be colored green and blue so that they stand out and you can find them easily. To understand the map properly, you need a **key** or **legend**. This explains the colors and **symbols** that have been used.

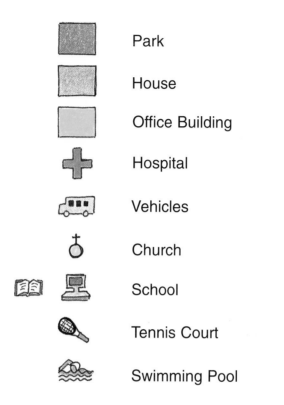

	Park
	House
	Office Building
	Hospital
	Vehicles
	Church
	School
	Tennis Court
	Swimming Pool

Some of the information has been omitted from the legend.

● **1.** Find the houses on the map. How many are there?

● **2.** Which building is the hospital?

● **3.** What could the blue closed curve represent?

Try drawing a map of your journey to school or to the shopping center. Make up your own colors and symbols for any special buildings or **landmarks** you pass. Remember to include a key.

Street Maps

Most towns publish a street map to help residents and visitors find their way around. As the name suggests, this concentrates on streets rather than buildings or **landmarks**. The streets are drawn as they appear from above.

Here are two street maps and two artist's impressions. Pair each map with its correct drawing.

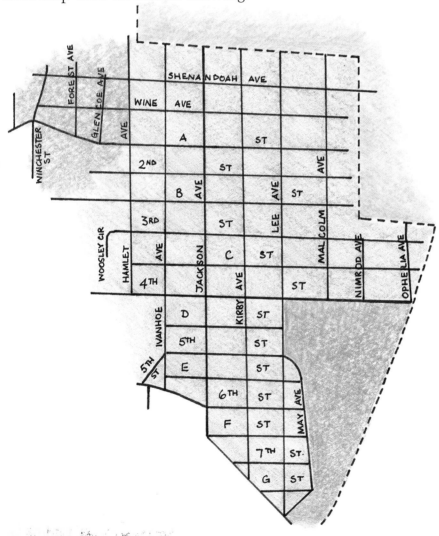

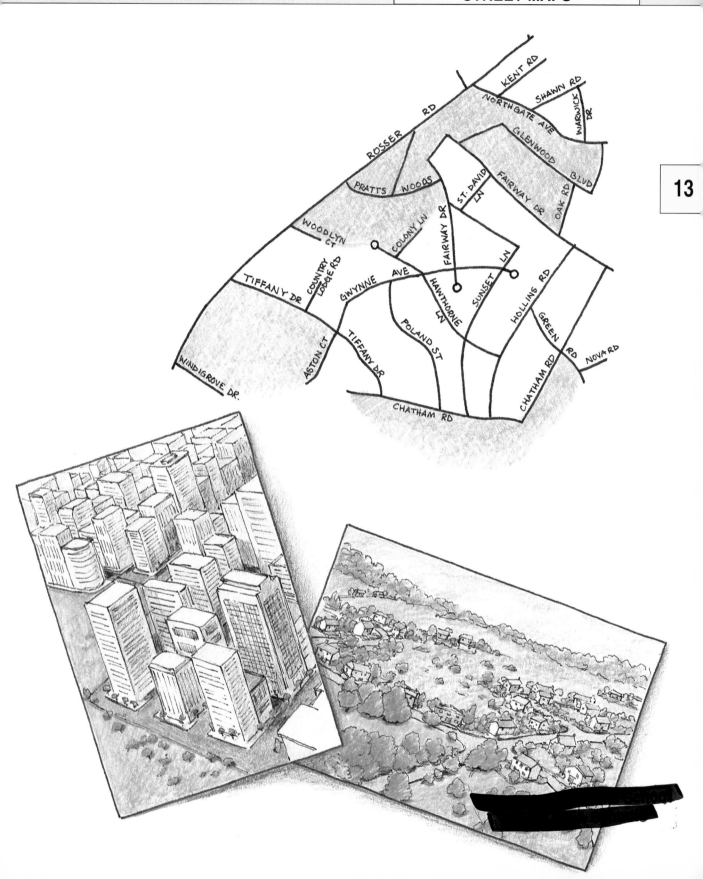

Grid References

When you are looking at a street map of a densely populated area, it can be difficult to find the particular road you are seeking. To make it easier, these maps are usually divided into a grid of squares.

You can see that the street map on the opposite page is divided into squares. It also has letters along the bottom and numbers up the left hand side. This allows each square to be identified by a letter and a number. Usually the letter of the square is given first, and then the number. This makes a kind of code that everyone understands. The letter and number for each square is called its **grid reference**.

● **1.** Write down on a piece of paper the codes for squares **(a)**, **(b)**, **(c)**, and **(d)** taken from the middle of a street map. The other squares have been given their codes to show you how the map works.

A street map usually includes a list, in alphabetical order, of all the streets and places that are shown on it. Each one is given its grid reference to make it easy to find on the map.

● **2.** What are the grid references of the building and streets shown on the map on page 15?

(a) White Oak Road
(b) Rossea Avenue
(c) Crofton Avenue
(d) Sidney Street
(e) Elementary School

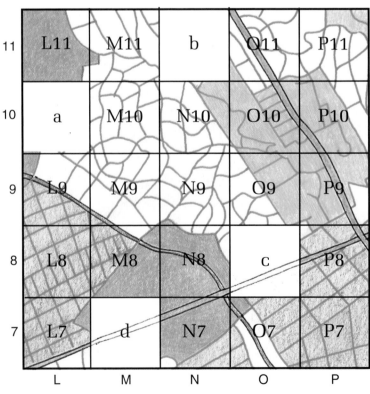

14

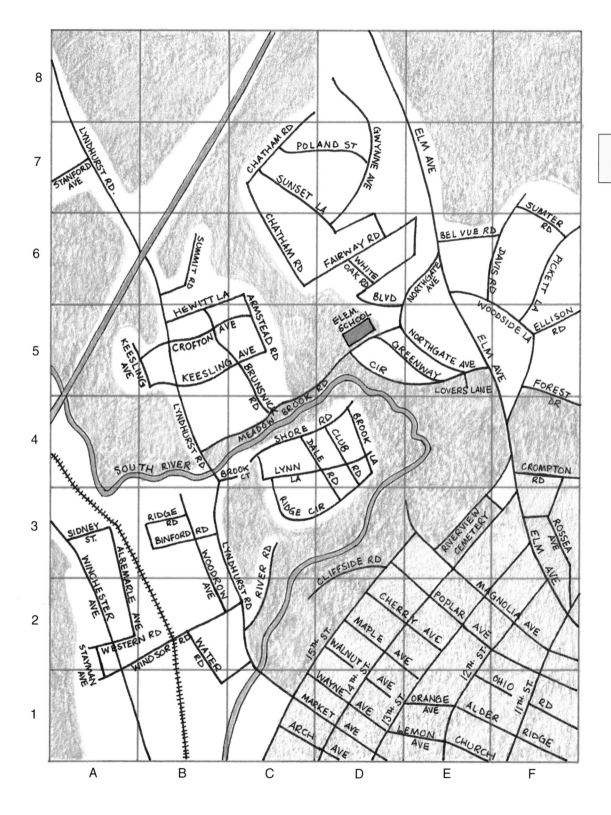

Take the first letters of each to find Treasure.

I6, C4, G4, C6 & D6,
J4 & J5, D3 & E3,
F5 & G5, D7 & E7,
G2 & H3, B7 & C7,
A4 & A5 & A6.

It is rumored that, many years ago, pirates' treasure was hidden on Treasure Island. An old parchment was found with the message shown on the left of this page.

● Use the map and the parchment to find out where the treasure is hidden.

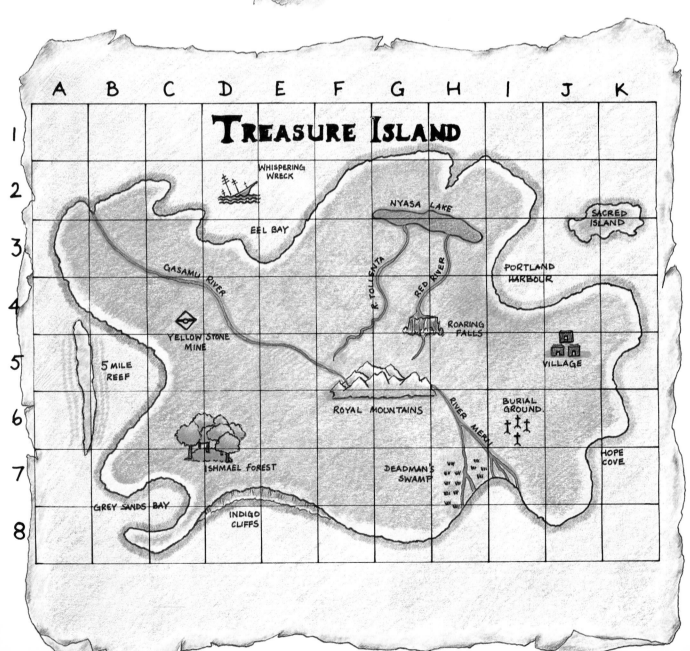

Theme park
a dice game for two or more players

You need two dice. On one of them, cover the dots on all the surfaces by sticking on pieces of paper labeled A to F. Each player needs a marker; you can use counters, buttons, pieces of different colored cardboard or paper, or anything that will fit on the squares of the game board. The score keeper needs a pencil and paper.

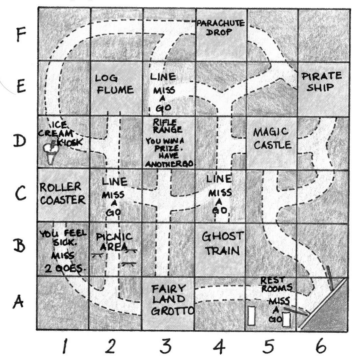

Take turns throwing the dice. The letter and number on the dice make a grid reference. Place your marker in the appropriate square in the grid. If there are instructions in the square, follow them. The object of the game is to visit as many of the attractions (colored pink) as possible. You score one for each visit. You can either decide a time limit or keep going until someone reaches an agreed score.

Try making up your own grid reference games.

Six Figure Grid References

Sometimes a more precise grid reference than simply the letter and number of the square is required. For instance, on the map of Treasure Island, there is a long stretch of river in G5, and it would be helpful to know more exactly where to start digging.

Some maps have their grid lines numbered rather than their squares. Shown below is part of a map of Virginia.

Notice that only numbers are used and that 0 is used as a marker for single digit numbers so that each line has a two-figure identification.

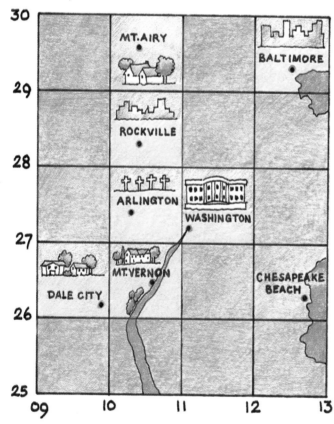

Find Washington on the map. It is a little way to the right of line 11 and above line 27. Imagine that the sides of the square where Washington is found are divided into tenths. You can now give a more precise explanation of Washington's position on the map. It is one tenth to the right of line 11 and two tenths up from line 27. This is given as the six-figure grid reference 111227. The three numbers of the across reference are called Eastings. The three numbers of the up reference are called Northings. The three Eastings numbers always come before the three Northings numbers in the grid reference.

● Three of these six figure grid references are definitely wrong. Find the places and write down on a piece of paper their corrected references.

Mt. Airy	104296
Baltimore	125293
Rockville	093284
Arlington	106272
Dale City	909226
Mt. Vernon	106265
Chesapeake Beach	127263

Finding the Way

When you are in surroundings where there are many **landmarks**, buildings, and roads, it is easy to find your way by following instructions to turn left or right at particular points. This does not work very well when you are exploring wide expanses of territory where few people live. The pioneers who traveled West to make a new life or to seek gold in the eighteenth and nineteenth **centuries** had to use other means to find their way.

It was even more difficult for fifteenth and sixteenth century European explorers and sailors such as Christopher Columbus and Ferdinand Magellan. They knew less about what lay ahead of them than an astronaut does today. There were few maps to help them. They were not even sure that the Earth was **spherical**. Some of the sailors were terrified that they would fall off the edge of the world if they sailed too far across the ocean.

Ferdinand Magellan

Vasco De Gama

Christopher Columbus

John Cabot

Hernando Cortes

But long before Columbus, people such as the ancestors of the North American Indians, the Polynesians, the Greeks, the Romans, the Vikings, the Arabs, and others had undertaken long journeys of exploration across snow, desert, forest, and sea.

They found their way by observing the positions of the stars at night and the sun by day. They noticed that the sun always rises in what we call the East and sets in what we call the West.

It may be the position of the sun that helps birds and animals such as caribou to **migrate** long distances. Animals and birds seem to make their journeys by **instinct**. They have a kind of in-built program that makes them respond automatically to **stimuli** such as changes of temperature, the length of the day, and the position of the sun in the sky.

People learn from each other how to plan journeys. We can learn from other people's experience and listen to their stories and advice. We can read the books they have written and the maps they have made. We can use our hands to make tools and instruments to help us measure distances and direction.

Christopher Columbus discovered the New World in his ship the *Santa Maria*. He charted his travels using his great kinowledge of winds, currents, and climates

Compass Directions

22

By using their skills, people have learned to **navigate**, or find their way, across the Earth and beyond. An important navigational instrument that was invented about one thousand years ago is the **compass**. This is usually a circular face containing a marked dial and a needle that swings freely. The needle is made from magnetic iron and will always point toward the north. It points at what is called magnetic north, which is not exactly the same as the North Pole.

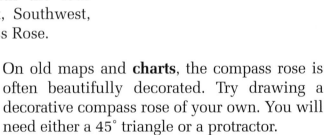

The inner part of the dial of a compass is usually marked with the four **cardinal** points of the compass, North, South, East, and West and with the four intermediate points, Northeast, Southest, Southwest, and Northwest. This is called the Compass Rose.

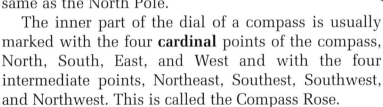

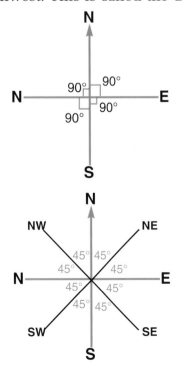

On old maps and **charts**, the compass rose is often beautifully decorated. Try drawing a decorative compass rose of your own. You will need either a 45° triangle or a protractor.

Draw a West to East line across the paper. Use the triangle or protractor to draw the North-South line at right angles to the West to East line. Check that the angles between North, East, South, and West are each 90°.

With the triangle or the protractor, measure 45° between North and East. Draw in the Southwest/Northeast line. Repeat between West and North for the Northwest/Southeast line. Check that each of the eight angles measures 45°. Label and decorate the eight points.

Making Your Own Compass

You need a bar magnet, a needle and a pin, a drinking straw, paper and glue, water, and a saucer.

Rub the needle with the magnet to magnetize it. This will take about thirty seconds. Rub in one direction only, not backwards and forwards. Test to see if your needle is magnetized by seeing if it will pick up a pin.

Mark North, South, East, and West on the **circumference** of the saucer with pieces of glued paper. Use a ruler and triangle to check that they are at **right angles**.

Cut the straw so that it is slightly shorter than the **diameter** of the saucer. Push the needle through the middle of the straw and at right angles to it to form a cross. Put some water in the saucer and float the needle and straw cross on it.

The needle will swing around and finally come to rest. Either the point or the eye will be pointing north. Think of where the sun sets – that is west. Turn the saucer so that the West label on the saucer is in approximately the correct direction. Continue gently turning the saucer until either the point or the eye of the needle is pointing at the North label.

It is important to keep your compass well away from any other magnetized object to get a true reading.

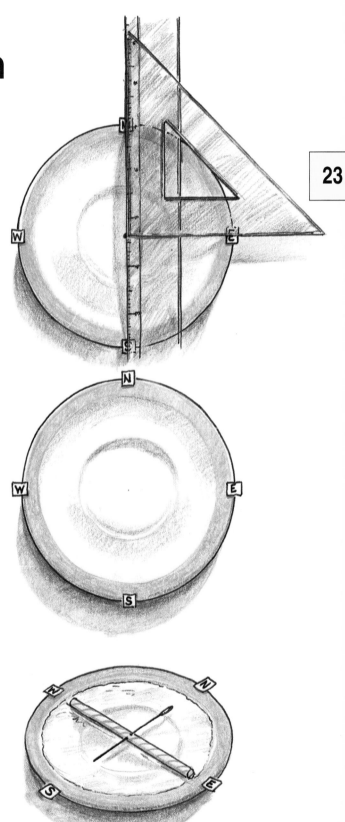

Using Compass Directions

The outer edge of the dial of a compass is marked off into 360 degrees.

This allows you to give very accurate and specific directions. You can say how many degrees clockwise from North the line that you have to take is to reach a particular point. This line is called a **bearing**.

You have to learn the relative positions of the four cardinal points of the compass. One way of remembering them is that when North is ahead of you, West and East are on your left and right respectively and their initials spell WE.

Sailors use intermediate points in between the eight points, such as North-Northeast and Northeast-East.

To find North with a compass, you turn the compass around until the North marked on the dial is underneath the point of the needle.

The direction of North is usually shown on a map. If you lay your compass on the map and line it up with the North marked on the map, you can tell in which direction you have to travel.

You can give directions in terms of the points of the compass. This robot is programmed to recognize North, South, East, and West. It is remote controlled and will continue along a given course until given the command N, S, E, or W. Then it

will turn and continue in the direction it has been given.
The robot has been sent into a building to check whether
there has been any structural damage after an earthquake.
These are the commands it was given. N, E, N, S, W, N, W, S,
N, E, N, S, W, E, N, W, E, S. The robot goes along the passages
and through the doors.

● Follow the directions to discover the message the robot
brought back.

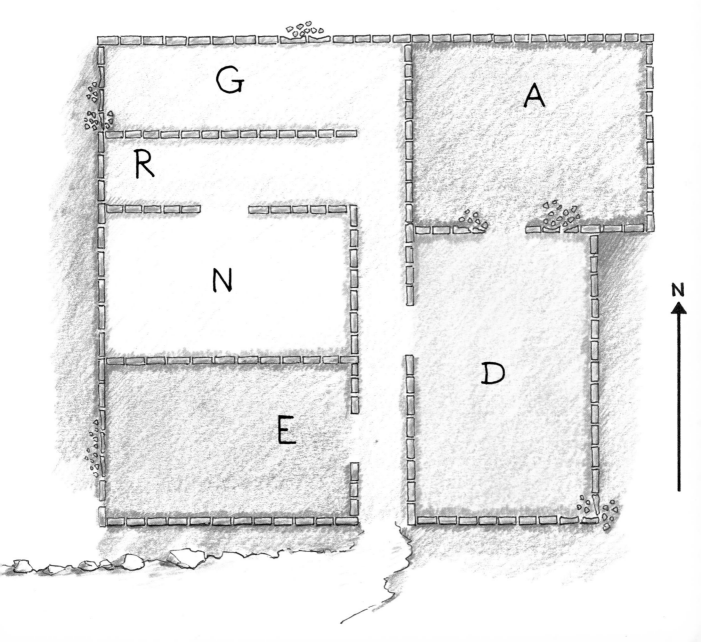

You can practice using the points of the compass as directions by blindfolding a partner and guiding him or her around an obstacle course of furniture using N, S, E, W, and STOP. Begin with your partner facing North.

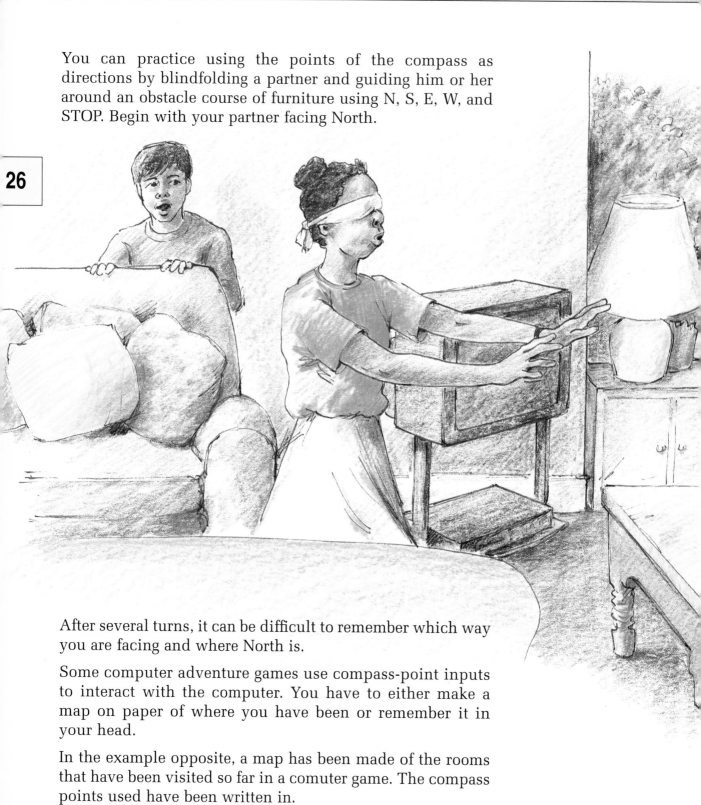

After several turns, it can be difficult to remember which way you are facing and where North is.

Some computer adventure games use compass-point inputs to interact with the computer. You have to either make a map on paper of where you have been or remember it in your head.

In the example opposite, a map has been made of the rooms that have been visited so far in a comuter game. The compass points used have been written in.

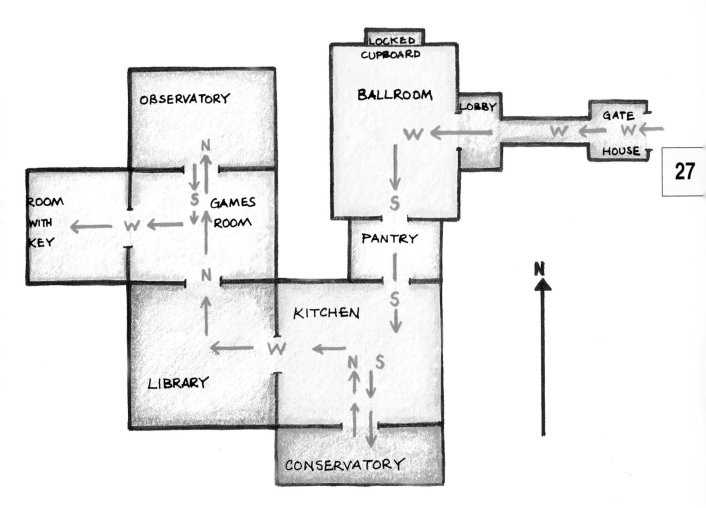

● **1.** When you have taken the key, what directions must you give the computer to get back to the locked cabinet?

When you unlock the cupboard, you find a secret staircase. You go up it into a panelled room, then West into a room which is empty except for a single shoe in one corner. You pick up the shoe and return to the panelled room. From there you go East and find an observatory with a glass domed roof. There is a door to the South. You enter it and find an **octagonal** shaped instrument room. A door to the West leads to a look out tower. You enter and are captured by a guard.

● **2.** Draw a map of your journey starting when you find herself in the panelled room.

Scales on Maps

The robot and blindfold game instructions only work because the person giving the instructions signals when it is time to change direction. This ship has to follow a channel marked on a **chart** in order to enter the harbor safely and avoid the hazards hidden beneath the water.

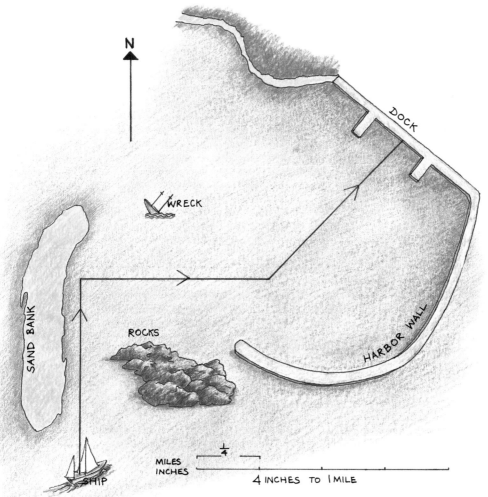

The pilot has to calculate how far the ship must travel in a particular direction before it has to change course. He does this by using the **scale** that is marked on the chart. In this case 1 inch on the chart is equivalent to ¼ mile on the sea.

The pilot's first two instructions are:
(1) North for ¾ mile and
(2) East for ¾ mile.

● **1.** Which of these is the correct third instruction?
(a) North for ½ mile
(b) Northwest for ¾ mile
(c) Northeast for ¾ mile
(d) Northeast for 1 mile

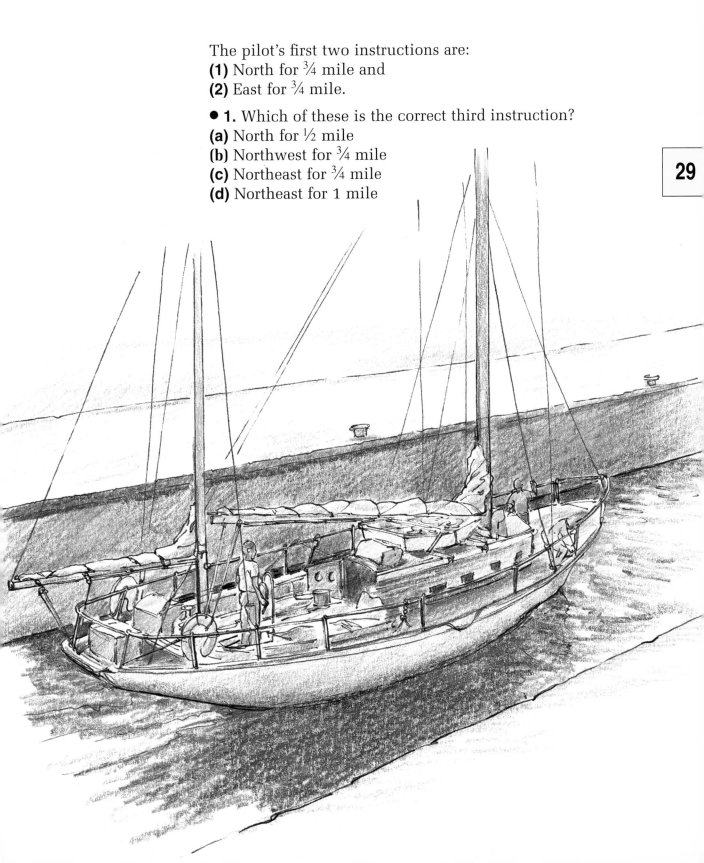

We need maps drawn to various scales according to what kind of journey we wish to make. Signora Petrie is planning a trip from Italy to visit her grandchildren in California. She needs a small scale map or **atlas**. The mapmaker has drawn each country so small that all of the Earth can be shown on one page.

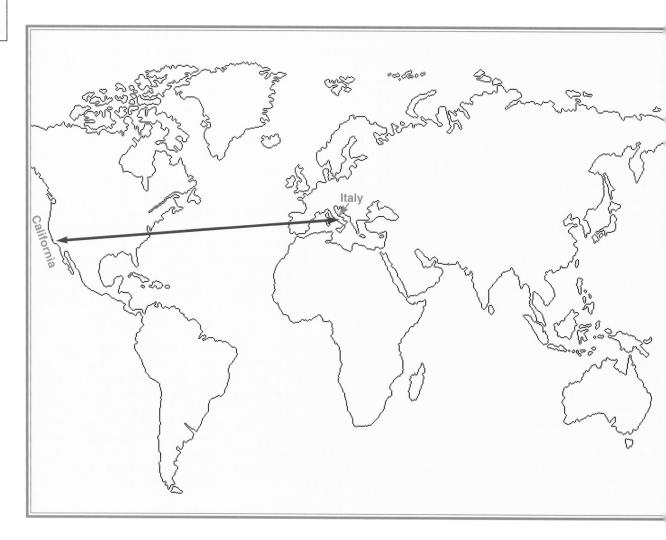

The Earth is a slightly distorted **sphere**, and a globe shows the true positions and sizes of the continents and countries in relation to each other. To help pinpoint positions on the Earth, a grid of lines is drawn on the globe. The lines that pass through the North and South poles are called lines of longitude, or meridians. The lines drawn around the globe from West to East are lines of latitude, or parallels.

Projections

A globe would be inconvenient to carry on a journey, so people have tried various ways of drawing accurate maps of the world on paper. A map drawn on a page is flat, so the mapmaker has to stretch some parts of the Earth and shrink others. He has to **project** a curved surface onto a flat one.

You can see the problem if you try to peel the skin from an orange in one piece. Here are two ways of doing it.

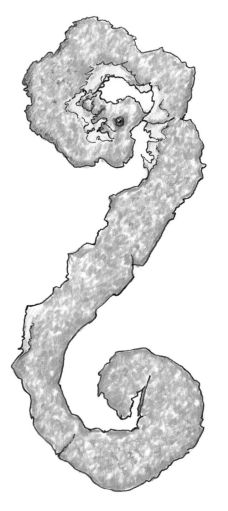

Can you find any more ways?

You can also try cutting a newspaper pattern in one piece to cover a ball.

These are some of the projections that mapmakers have made. You may have done something similar to Mercator's projection with your orange peel or newspaper.

Mercator's projection is named after its inventor, a Dutchman of the 16th century. He invented the system of projecting maps of the globe on to a cylinder and drawing the meridians of longitude at right angles to the parallels of latitude as straight lines.

34

Goode's projection

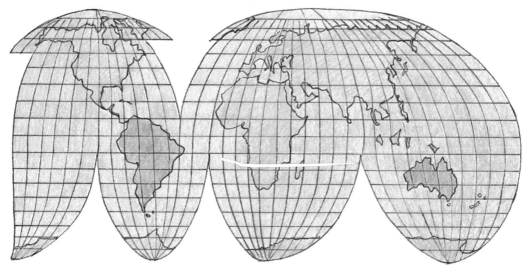

Stereographic projection

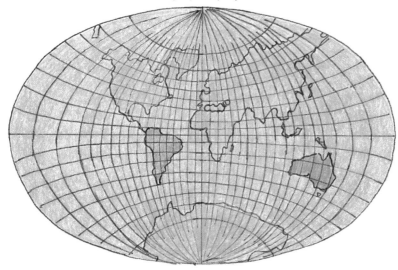

If you look at the relative sizes of South America and Australia in Goode's and the stereographic projections, you can see that they have been stretched and shrunk differently. On the stereographic projection, South America and Australia are about the same size. On Goode's projection, South America is about twice as large as Australia.

● **1.** Which projection gives the most accurate idea of the relative sizes of South America and Australia?

Each projection has advantages and disadvantages.

Draw an 8-inch square. Divide it into a grid of one-inch squares. Copy the figure that has been drawn on the grid below onto the grid you have made.

● **2.** What happens?

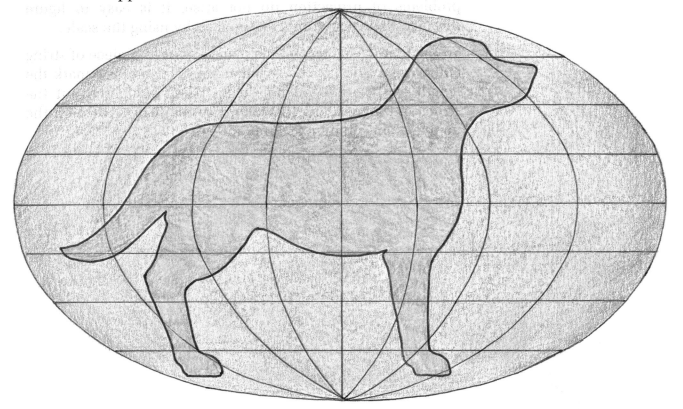

Calculating Distances from Scales

36

Marcus is planning two circular routes for a charity walk-a-thon in his neighborhood. He will need a large scale map with all the streets and sidewalks marked. The large scale will make it easier to calculate the distance of the route as well.

When the map is large scale, the amount of curvature of the Earth in the area covered by the map is small, and the problems of **projection** do not arise. It is easy to figure distances between points on the map by using the scale.

To calculate distances from a map, you need a piece of string and a ruler. You lay the string along the route and mark the length of the route on the string. Then straighten out the string and lay it along the ruler. Use the scale shown on the map to change the inches into miles.

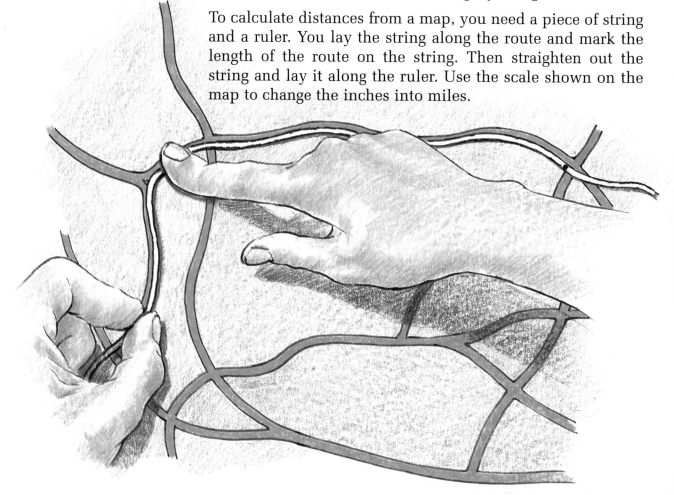

You can make a rough estimate using your thumb. The length of your top thumb joint is roughly an inch. You can count off along the route with your thumb joint and use the scale to work out the distance.

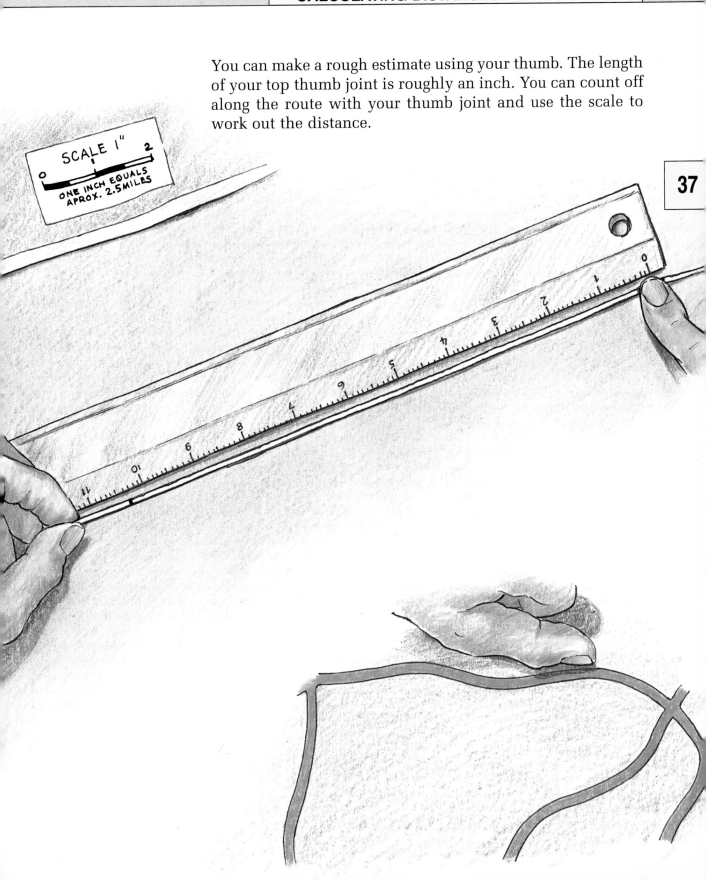

CALCULATING DISTANCES FROM SCALES

Marcus has planned a two-mile route and a twenty-mile route and marked them on the map.

● Has he figured them correctly?
Measure the route accurately.

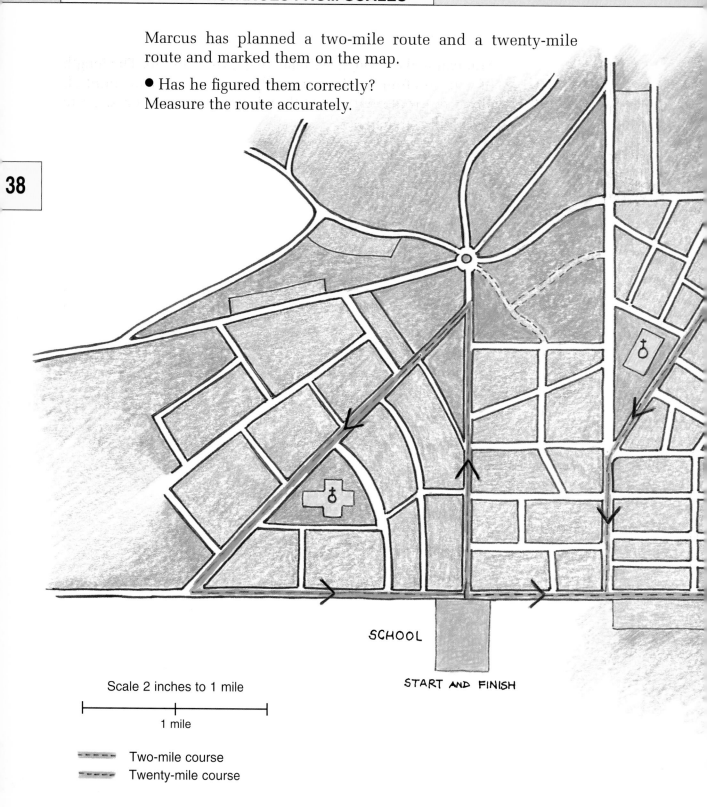

Scale 2 inches to 1 mile

1 mile

- - - - Two-mile course
- - - - Twenty-mile course

SCHOOL

START AND FINISH

Scale Drawing

In many situations it is useful to make a scale drawing. When an architect designs a building, she makes scale drawings of the site as well as of the exterior and interior of the building. She must use a different scale for each of these.

● Which will be drawn to the smallest scale: the site, the outside of the building, the interior floor plan of the whole building, or individual room plans?

Scale drawings can be used to show things either larger or smaller than life. A picture of an integrated circuit in an electronics textbook might show it as much larger than it really is. This will enable you to see the details of its components. A larger than life-size drawing is called an enlargement. When you look at a scale drawing, you need to know the scale in order to understand the picture fully.

Scale can be shown in different ways. Sometimes an object whose size you know will be placed alongside the object drawn to scale. Alternatively, a ruled line can be drawn that shows two sets of measurements like this:

A colon is sometimes used. Scale 1 : 20 means that each length in the drawing is $\frac{1}{20}$ of the actual length.

● Rita's dad makes dollhouse furniture. He is making a scale model of this antique sofa. The length of the seat is 60″. At a scale of 1 : 20, how long will the seat of the model be?

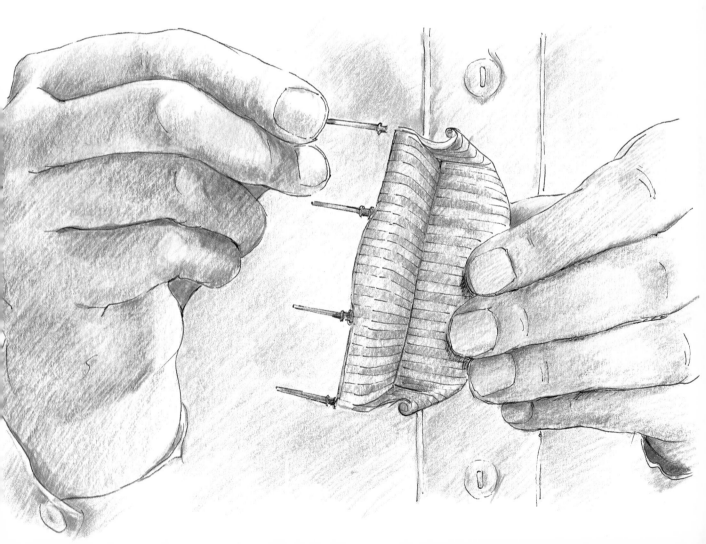

Emily's Letter Rack

Andrea has decided to make a letter rack as a Christmas present for her friend, Emily. She has made a drawing of how she wants it to look.

In order to figure out how much wood she needs, Andrea makes half-scale drawings of each of the pieces she needs to use to make the rack. Each length on the drawing is half the length it will be on the rack.

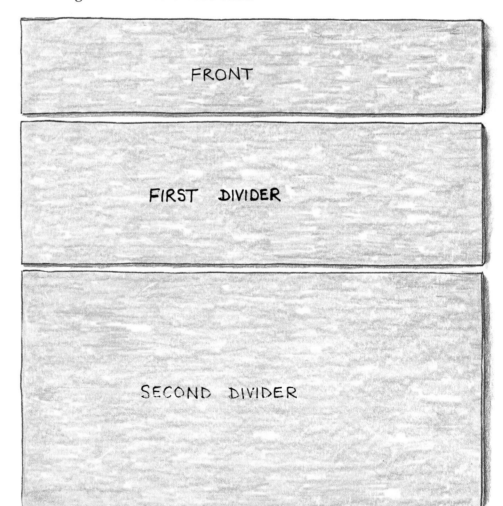

FRONT

FIRST DIVIDER

SECOND DIVIDER

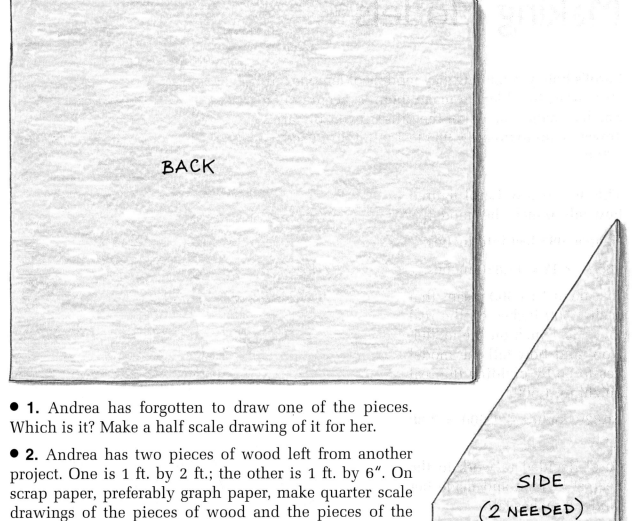

BACK

SIDE
(2 NEEDED)

● **1.** Andrea has forgotten to draw one of the pieces. Which is it? Make a half scale drawing of it for her.

● **2.** Andrea has two pieces of wood left from another project. One is 1 ft. by 2 ft.; the other is 1 ft. by 6″. On scrap paper, preferably graph paper, make quarter scale drawings of the pieces of wood and the pieces of the rack. One foot will be drawn as 3″, 6″ as 1½″ and so on. Divide each length by 4 to make a quarter-scale drawing.

Cut out the pieces. Try to fit the scale drawings of the pieces of the rack onto the scale drawings of the pieces of wood.

It is a good idea to make as few cuts as possible to save work.

● **3.** Does Andrea have enough wood?

Making Models

Carol's hobby is making clay models of famous buildings and structures. She likes to make them as accurately as she can. She has made a model of the Eiffel Tower in Paris. The Eiffel Tower is approximately 985 feet tall. Carol used a scale of 1 : 1,500.

This is the way Carol figured how tall to make her model.

Change 985 feet into inches.

985 ft. × 12 = 11,820 inches.

A scale of 1 : 1,500 means that each 1,500 inches on the real tower is 1 inch on the model. Now find how tall the model has to be by dividing the real height by 1,500.

11,820 inches ÷ 1,500 = 7.88 inches.

Carol decided to work to the nearest ½ inch and made her model 8 inches tall.

44

Carol has also made a model, to the same scale, of the Empire State Building in New York. This model is 10 inches high. Here is a way you can figure approximately how high the Empire State Building is:

The actual building is 1,500 times larger than the model.

1,500 × 10" = 15,000"
15,000" ÷ 12 = 1,250 ft.

The Empire State Building is approximately 1,250 feet tall. Remember that Carol builds her models to the nearest ½" and is using a very small scale.

45

This model village is made on a scale of 1 to 10.

● **1.** An average house is about 22 feet tall. About how tall are the model houses?

● **2.** The river in the model is 48" wide. How wide is the actual river?

● **3.** Approximately how tall are the model people?

46

Ralph is making a scale model of a North American Harvard, a World War II trainer plane. The model is made to a scale of 1 : 72. The wing span of the model is 7".

● **4.** What is the wingspan of a North American Harvard?

● **5.** The length of a North American Harvard is 28½ ft. How long will the model be?

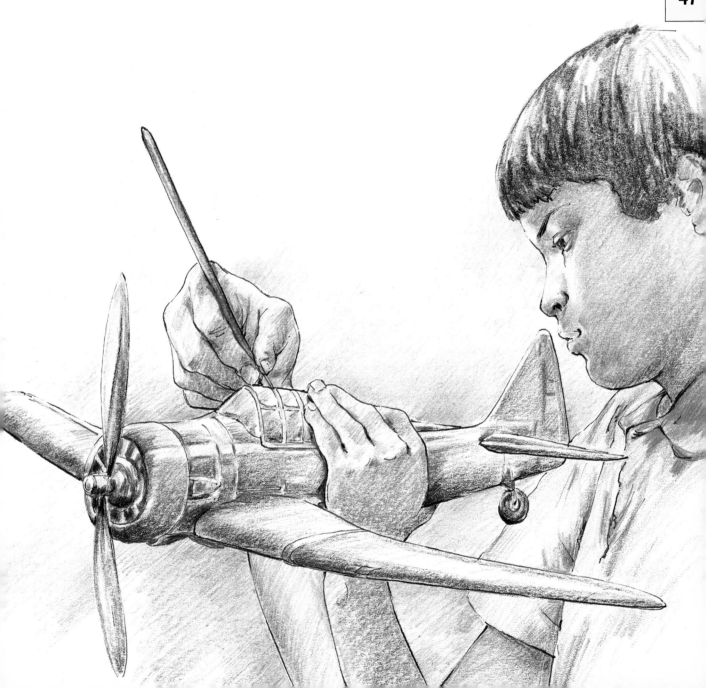

Planning a Room

Henry's mom is always complaining about his messy bedroom. She has offered to buy him a storage unit and a computer work station to make it easier to organize his room.

The problem is how to fit all the furniture into the room. Henry already has a closet, a bed, a chair, and a chest of drawers. The room is 8 feet, 6 inches at its widest point and 9 feet, 6 inches long.

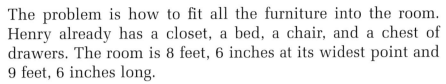

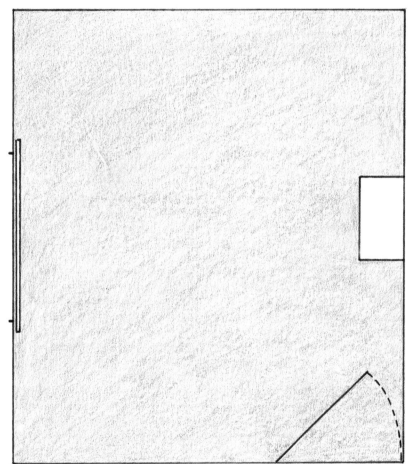

Henry decides that the easiest way to plan the room is to make scale drawings of the room and of all the furniture. He can then move the drawings of the furniture around the plan of the room to find the best arrangement. The room and the furniture must all be drawn to the same scale.

This is Henry's first idea.

50

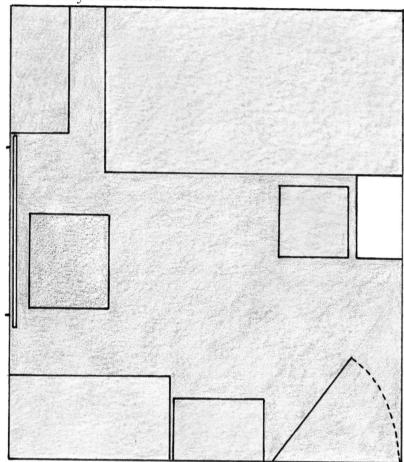

● **1.** What is wrong with the position of the chest of drawers?

● **2.** Make your own plan of your solution to Henry's problem. You can use the same scale as Henry if you wish or, if you have a large sheet of paper, you can use a bigger scale. One inch : 1 foot is easy to calculate.

Remember to leave room to open doors and drawers and to get in and out of bed. Do not stand tall furniture in front of the window.

Finding Lengths by Scale Drawing

Sometimes you can use scale drawing to find a distance that is difficult to measure.

Judy and Colin are arguing about how high their kite is flying. Judy says it is 150 feet up; Colin figures it is more like 300 feet.

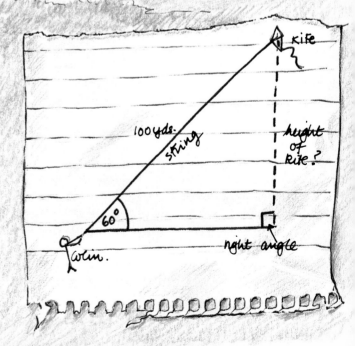

Judy decides to make a scale drawing. She knows that the string is 100 yards long and it is all unwound from the holder. She estimates that the string is making an angle of 60° with the ground. First Judy makes a sketch of the situation.

She decides that a scale of 1 inch : 20 yards will give her a reasonably sized drawing. She uses a protractor and triangle to make a scale drawing.

This is the accurate scale drawing that Judy made.

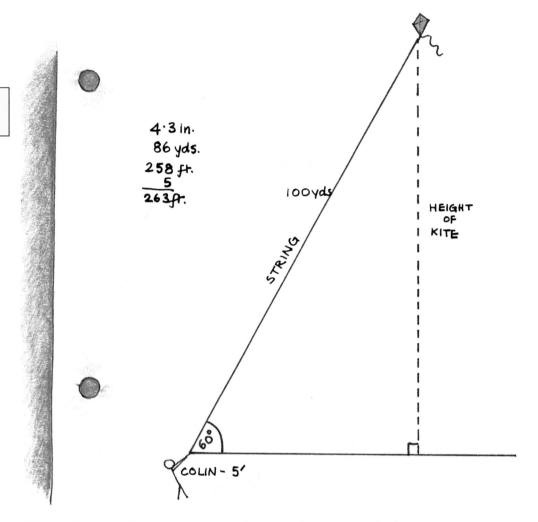

4·3 in.
86 yds.
258 ft.
  5
263 ft.

100 yds

STRING

HEIGHT
OF
KITE

60°

COLIN – 5'

52

Now she needs to measure the height of the kite in her drawing. It measures 4.3 inches. She multiplies by 20 to change this into the real height in yards.

$4.3 \times 20 = 86$

The height of the kite is 86 yards above Colin's hand. Judy needs to add on about another 5 feet for the height of Colin's arm above the ground.

● Whose estimate was closest to the real height?

Judy estimated the angle that the string made with the ground. This angle is called the **angle of elevation**. If a surveyor needs an angle of elevation in order to find a height, he uses a theodolite to measure the angle accurately.

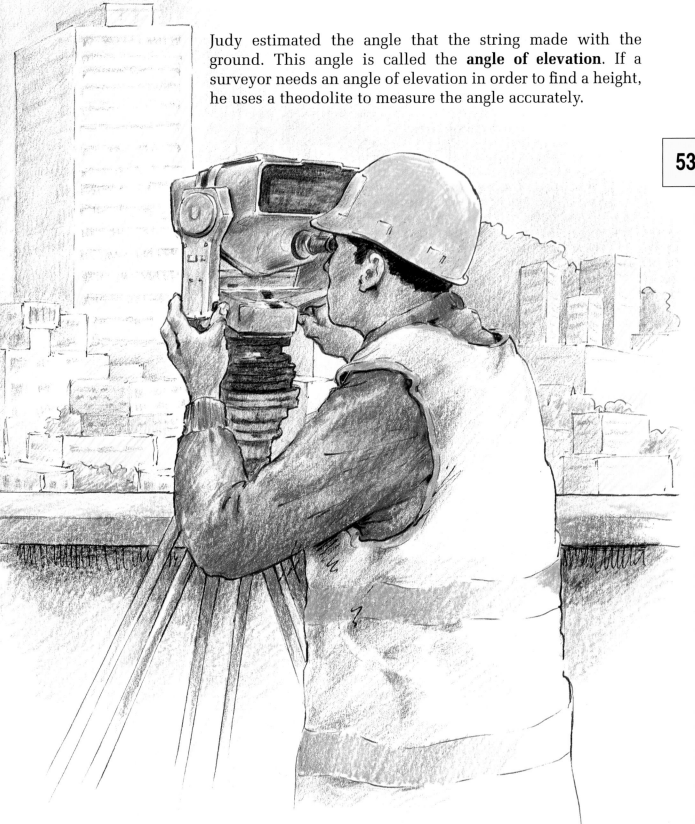

● **1.** A plane is climbing at an angle of elevation of 25°. How much higher is it when it has traveled 3 miles?

Make a sketch and then a scale drawing. Use a scale of 1 inch to 3 miles.

54

A man on top of a cliff 300 feet high is in line with two ships whose **angles of depression** are 30° and 40°. The angles of depression are the angles between the horizontal and the lines from the man to the ships.

● **2.** By scale drawing, find the distance between the ships. Ignore the height of the man.

An Offset Survey

Ruth's mom loves to garden. She has been given a virtual reality package for her computer to help her design her garden and set up a database of the plants that grow in it. The first stage in using the program is to input the dimensions of the garden to enable the computer to draw a plan of it.

Ruth shows her mom how to do an offset survey of the garden so that she can make an accurate plan of it. This method is not as accurate as the method mapmakers use. Mapmakers draw maps by using instruments to measure distances and angles so they can plot triangles of land and fit them together.

An offset survey uses a base line and **perpendicular** measurements from it. The advantage of the offset survey is that you do not need an instrument to measure angles. It is important, however, that you take your measurements at right angles to the base line. If you have a piece of cardboard with sides of 3 or 4 feet and a right angle at the corner, you can use that as a check.

Alternatively, you can do as the ancient Egyptian surveyors did, and knot a 12-foot length of string at 3 feet and 4 feet to make a 3, 4, 5 triangle. When you join the ends and pull it taut, it makes a right-angled triangle.

KNOT

5 FT.

4 FT.

RIGHT ANGLE

3 FT

KNOT

ENDS JOINED

The first stage is to draw a rough plan of the garden. Ruth has to draw the approximate shape of the plot and its boundaries. Then she needs to mark in fixed features such as trees, the pond, and the shed.

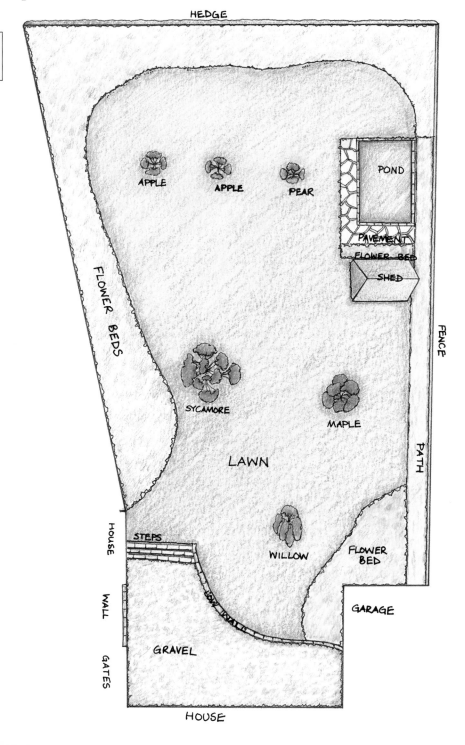

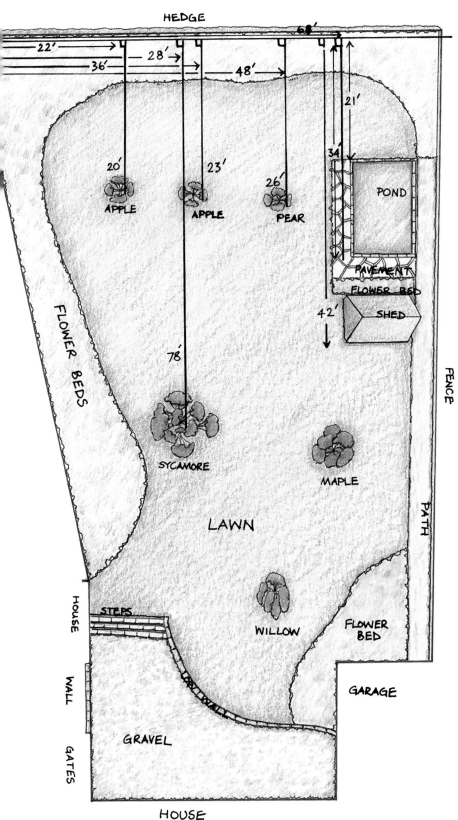

The next stage is to decide on the base line. Ruth decides to use the bottom boundary as the base line, as this is a straight line across the garden at it widest point.

Ruth and her mom use a 60-foot tape measure and a knotted string to measure from the base line to the points shown on the opposite page. They carefully record each measurement on the sketch plan. If you do not have a long tape measure you can measure a 60-foot length of string with a ruler and then use that.

The final stage is to make an accurate plan. Ruth looks at the measure-ments and decides that a scale of 1 inch to 16 feet will give a drawing that will fit onto a letter sized sheet of paper. She draws the base line to scale. Then she uses a triangle to lightly draw in the offset measurements.

Glossary

angle of elevation   the angle that a line drawn from an observer to an object above makes with the horizontal. When the object is below the observer, the angle is called the angle of depression.

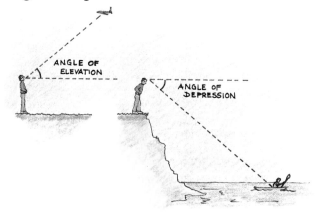

atlas   a book of maps or charts. In Greek mythology, Atlas was the god who held the world on his shoulders. In times past, his picture was shown on the front of an atlas.

cardinal   the cardinal points of the compass are North, South, East, and West. In general, "cardinal" means something basic and important.

century   a period of one hundred years. We are living in the twentieth century.

chart   a map used for navigating around the coast and at sea

circumference   the distance around the edge of a circle

conical projection   a map projection drawn as if a cone of paper has been placed over the globe touching it along one line of latitude

compass   an instrument with a needle that always points toward the magnetic north

diameter   the distance through the center of a circle from one point on its circumference to another

grid reference   the combination of numbers, or the number and letter, that represents the position of a particular object or place in a grid of lines

key   the explanation of symbols and colors that have been used on a map

landmark   a building or geographical feature that is well known and easily seen

legend   the explanation of symbols and colors that have been used on a map; same as "key"

Mercator   a cylindrical projection made as though the globe has been wrapped in a cylinder of paper

migrate   to travel from one place to another; often used to describe the yearly journeys made by birds and animals in search of food and a good climate

navigate   to find the way by using the sun, stars, landmarks, and special instruments

octagonal   eight sided

perpendicular   line at right angles to another

projection   the process of transferring a curved image onto a flat surface

right angle   an angle of 90°; a quarter turn. The four corners of this page are all right angles.

scale   a means of telling you how much larger or smaller a drawing of an object is than the object itself

sphere   a figure, such as a ball or globe, in which every point on its surface is the same distance from the center

stimulus   something that triggers a reaction

stereographic projection   a projection of the Earth as viewed from a point on its surface and imagining it flattened into a disk.

symbol   a drawing or sign that stands for something else; for example a circle with a cross on it is often used on maps as a symbol for a church with a steeple

59

Answers

Page 7

Tammy lives on Rowlands Drive.

Page 8

1. Maria has gone to church.

2. Alvin and Jean should turn right.

3. You would need to say something like, "Turn RIGHT out of the apartments, walk to the end of Rowlands Drive. Turn RIGHT up Haddington Street, passing three houses on your LEFT. Turn LEFT into Elm Drive, which is the first turn on your left. The bus stop is a little way along, on the LEFT."

4. Stand with your back to the dead end. Walk to the T intersection. Turn LEFT. Ignore the first turn on your left and walk to the end of the path. Turn LEFT. Turn RIGHT at the T intersection. Keep going to the dead end and turn LEFT. Turn LEFT again at the next dead end. Do not go into the middle, turn RIGHT. Ignore the next turn on the RIGHT, go on to the dead end, and turn RIGHT. Turn RIGHT at the next dead end. Ignore the next LEFT turn, turn RIGHT at the next two dead ends, turn LEFT, ignore the next right turn, and turn RIGHT at the dead end.

5. This is a copy of the maze with the route marked.

FINISH

START

Directions are R, L, L, R, R, L, L, L, L, R, R, R, R, L, L.

Page 11

1. There are 15 houses.

2. The hospital is the building with a red cross on it.

3. The blue closed shape represents a pond.

Page 14

1. (a) L10 **(b)** N11 **(c)** O8 **(d)** M7

2. (a) D6 **(b)** F3 **(c)** B5 **(d)** A3 **(e)** D5

Page 16

I6 Burial ground

C4 Yellowstone Mine

G4 Roaring Falls

C6 and D6 Ishmael Forest

J4 and J5 Village

D3 and E3 Eel Bay

F5 and G5 Royal Mountains

D7 and E7 Indigo Cliffs

G2 and H3 Nyasa Lake

B7 and C7 Graysands Bay

A4, A5 and A6 Five Mile Reef

B Y R I V E R I N G 5 (By river in G5)

Page 19

Rockville 104283

Arlington 103274

Dale City 099262

Page 25

The message was DANGER

Page 27

1. E, (Game Room) S, (Library) E, (Kitchen) N, (Pantry) N, (Ballroom)

2. Your map should look something like this . The room sizes do not matter but they should be in the same order. `

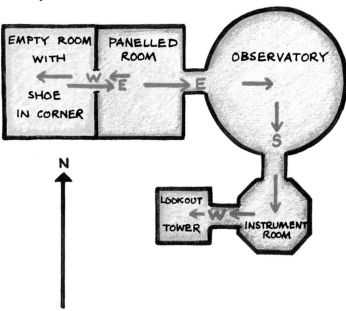

Page 29

1. (c)

Page 34

1. Goode's projection is the more accurate.

2. Your figure should look like this.

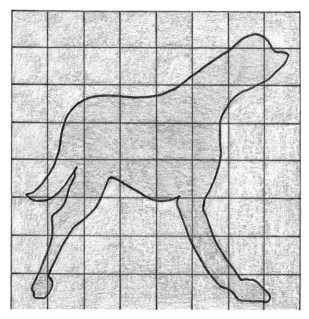

Some parts have shrunk and some have stretched.

Page 38

Marcus has made the two-mile course too long. It measures five inches, not four. The quickest way to check is to mark four inches and twenty inches on a piece of string and see if the routes fit.

Page 40

The site plans.

Page 41

3″

Pages 42 and 43

1. Andrea has forgotten the base.
2. This is one solution. It has the advantage that the number of cuts required is as few as possible.

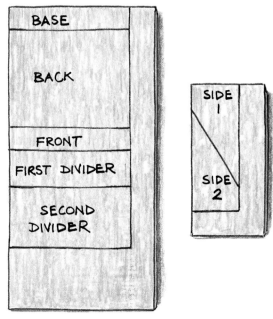

3. Yes

Pages 46 and 47

1. About 26″ or 27″ (22 ft. = 264″ 264″ ÷10 = 26.4″
2. 40 ft. (48″ × 10 = 480″)
3. Between 6½″ and 7″
(The average height for women is about 5 ft. 6″   66″ ÷ 10 = 6.6″
The average height for men is about 6 ft. 72″ ÷ 10 = 7.2″)
4. 42 ft. (72 x 7″= 504″   504″÷ 12 = 42 ft.)
5. 4¾″ (28½ ft. × 12 = 342″ 342″ ÷ 72 = 4 ¾″)

Page 50

1. Henry has not left enough room to stand and open the drawers in the chest.
2. This is one way of arranging Henry's room, but there are others.

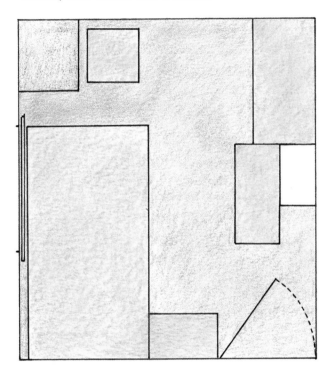

Page 52

Charlie's estimate was best. From the scale drawing the kite was 263 feet above the ground. (86 yards = 258 feet).

Page 54

1. Your scale drawing should look like this.

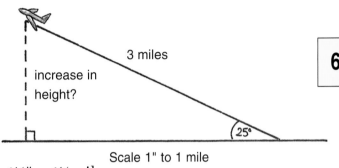

Scale 1" to 1 mile

$1\frac{1}{2}$" = $1\frac{1}{4}$ miles
$\quad = 1.25 \times 3 \times 176$
$\quad = 6{,}600$ ft.

2. The distance between the ships is $1\frac{3}{8}$ inches, which represents $127\frac{1}{2}$ feet ($\frac{1}{8}$ of $100 = 12\frac{1}{2}$).

Index

64